W9-CLO-030

Soldering

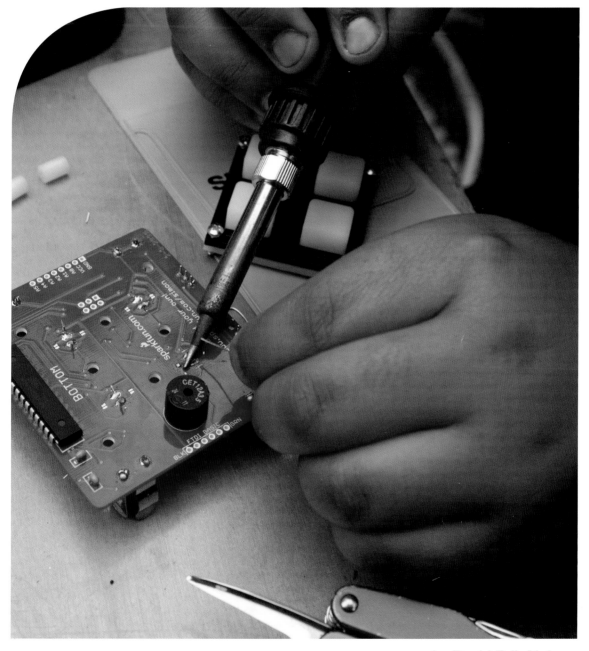

CHERRY LAKE PUBLISHING • ANN ARBOR, MICHIGAN

by **David Erik Nelson**

A Note to Adults: Please review the instructions for the activities in this book before allowing children to do them. Be sure to help them with any activities you do not think they can safely complete on their own.

A Note to Kids: Be sure to ask an adult for help with these activities when you need it. Always put your safety first!

Published in the United States of America by Cherry Lake Publishing
Ann Arbor, Michigan
www.cherrylakepublishing.com

Series editor: Kristin Fontichiaro

Photo Credits: Cover and page 1, hudson/www.flickr.com/CC BY-SA 2.0; page 4, stoic/www.flickr.com/CC BY 2.0; page 5, meddygarnet/ www.flickr.com/CC BY 2.0; page 7, lungstruck/www.flickr.com/ CC BY 2.0; page 9, norro/en.wikipedia.org/CC BY-SA 3.0; page 10 KevinHadley/en.wikipedia.org/CC BY-SA 3.0; page 11, oskay/ www.flickr.com/CC BY 2.0; page 12, tonnerrelombard/www.flickr.com/ CC BY 2.0; page 14, SparkFunElectronics/www.flickr.com/CC BY 2.0; page 18, Myself248/www.flickr.com/CC BY-SA 2.0; page 20, Solarbotics/ www.flickr.com/CC BY 2.0; page 22, makerbot/www.flickr.com/CC BY 2.0; pages 24, 26, and 27, David Erik Nelson, page 32, Justin Lundquist.

Library of Congress Cataloging-in-Publication Data
Nelson, David Erik, author.
 Soldering / by David Erik Nelson.
   pages cm. — (21st Century skills innovation library. Makers as innovators)
 Includes bibliographical references and index.
 ISBN 978-1-63137-774-7 (lib. bdg.) — ISBN 978-1-63137-794-5 (pbk.) — ISBN 978-1-63137-834-8 (e-book) —ISBN 978-1-63137-814-0 (pdf)
 1. Solder and soldering—Juvenile literature. 2. Metal-work—Juvenile literature. I. Title. II. Series: 21st century skills innovation library. Makers as innovators.
 TS610.N45 2015
 671.5'6—dc23   2014005538

Cherry Lake Publishing would like to acknowledge the work of The Partnership for 21st Century Skills. Please visit www.p21.org for more information.

Printed in the United States of America
Corporate Graphics Inc.
July 2014

Contents

Chapter 1

What Is Soldering?

H ave you ever looked inside a computer, a TV, a garage door opener, or some other electronic device? If so, you've probably noticed that these devices are full of electronic **components**. These bits and pieces are the parts that make an electronic device work. They are connected in **circuits**, or paths, through which electricity can flow.

A computer tower is filled with wires and electronic components.

You can use soldering to modify or create your own electronics.

The connections between components have to last a long time, even if the device gets knocked around a little. They also need to be able to be disconnected, so that parts can be repaired, replaced, or upgraded later. **Soldering** is a method of connecting components in a strong yet reversible way.

Soldering is a little like welding. Welding is the process of melting two or more pieces of metal together. The melted metal hardens as it cools.

This makes for a strong connection that will last a long time. Car bodies are welded. So are the beams that support skyscrapers. It is hard to take something apart once it has been welded.

Like welding, soldering joins pieces together using melted metal. However, it does not melt the objects themselves. Instead, a soft metal called solder is melted over the area where the objects will be joined. Solder melts at a lower temperature than the metal used to make electronic components. This means that the components themselves do not

Mighty Makers

If you like to build things, take them apart, repair them, or improve them, you might be a **maker**. Makers are creative people who are curious about the way things work. They use a wide variety of skills and tools to complete projects and learn new things. A makerspace is a place where makers come together to share ideas, tools, and skills. Sometimes, these spaces are called by other names, such as hackerspaces, guilds, clubs, or studios.

It is very common to see people soldering when you visit a makerspace. Soldering isn't just for building electronic devices. It is used in a wide variety of do-it-yourself projects and home repairs. Jewelry makers, sculptors, and plumbers all use different styles of soldering in their work.

melt when the solder is heated. As the solder cools and hardens, it forms a bond, or strong connection, between the components. Because solder is metal, it also **conducts** electricity and lasts a long time— unless you decide to make some changes.

Sometimes electronic parts are connected to a thin sheet called a circuit board. Look at the board's back to see where the pieces were soldered.

Look closely at the inside of an electronic device. You should see the points where components were soldered together. Almost all of the solder points you see in household devices were created by machines in big factories. But soldering was once a common skill taught in schools. Many people soldered components by hand. Building electronic devices was a popular hobby for both children and adults. As electronics became more common in everyday life, people became more interested in using brand-new gizmos and less interested in building them.

Today, soldering is once again becoming a popular skill. There are a lot of great do-it-yourself (DIY) electronics kits and projects available online. They range from very simple (and inexpensive) radios, toys, and audio equipment to complicated robots, home security systems, and more.

Chapter 2

Soldering Tools

The most important tool you'll need for soldering projects is called a soldering iron. There are many different types of soldering irons. Some are shaped like guns. These types of irons are not good for beginners. The best soldering irons for beginners are ones shaped like pencils. These can be purchased at most hardware stores and electronics hobby shops. Quality soldering irons made by well-known companies will cost a bit more than other models. However, they will work better and last longer. They are also much easier to learn to use.

A soldering iron is a tool used to melt solder so it can be applied to metals and form a bond.

The dark spot at the center of this wire is the wire's rosin core.

Just as there are many kinds of soldering irons, there are also many kinds of solder. For electronics projects, you can use rosin-core solder. This solder is made of a mixture of tin and lead. You can also use solder that is marked as "lead-free" or "silver-bearing." These types of solder are becoming more common because lead is bad for your health and for the environment. Lead-based rosin-core solder is still safe to use and handle, however. Just be sure to wash your hands after soldering. Standard rosin-core solder, lead-free solder, and silver-bearing solder all work equally well for hobby electronics.

Make sure not to get acid-core solder. This type of solder is used for plumbing and metalworking. It is

Check the label on a spool of soldering wire to find out what kind of wire it is.

not good for electronics projects. If you're confused by the selection of solders at the store, tell the staff there that you're doing an electronics project. They will be able to point you in the right direction.

You'll also need a small sponge. You can even use an old scrap of a larger sponge. It should be about the size of a packet of Saltine crackers. You'll use this sponge to clean the tip of your soldering iron as you work. It will get pretty gross and crusty, so you shouldn't use the sponge for anything except soldering.

Keep your soldering iron in a stand when you're not using it.

Optional Tools

In addition to solder, a soldering iron, and a sponge, there are several other tools that can be helpful when building electronics projects. The first is a stand for your soldering iron. You need a place to set the soldering iron when you're not using it. You don't want to set it on your table. The heat would burn the table's surface.

A set of wire strippers can also be useful. Wire strippers can cut through the plastic **insulation** of an electrical wire without harming the metal inside. If you don't have wire strippers, you can usually remove the insulation from wires using a small pair of scissors. This is a bit more challenging than using wire strippers. Doing it correctly takes some practice. Be careful not to nick the metal part of the wire. Damaging the metal will make it more likely to break later.

Another handy tool for electronics projects is a pair of needle-nose pliers. These small pliers have long, skinny tips. This allows them to grip tiny components. Most needle-nose pliers also have a built-in set of wire cutters, making them a very handy two-in-one tool.

A roll of electrical tape is helpful for many projects. This black, rubberized tape is long lasting and great for securing wires together. It is also handy for quick repairs, such as holding a battery case closed when it keeps popping open. Electrical tape sticks to plastic and metal better than Scotch tape does. It is less messy than duct tape and holds up better than masking tape.

A desoldering tool is useful when you need to take soldered connections apart. There are several types of desoldering tools. Solder suckers, which are also called desoldering pumps or desoldering bulbs, are like small vacuums with heat-resistant plastic tips. They are the easiest desoldering tools to use. You'll learn more about desoldering in the next chapter.

Chapter 3

How to Solder

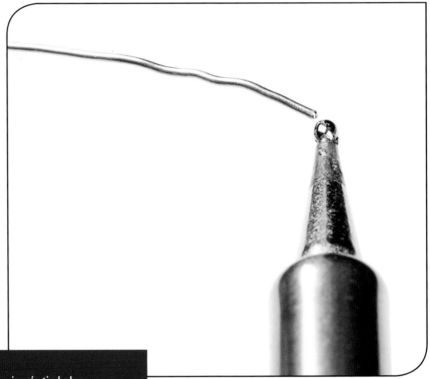

Adding solder to a soldering iron's tip helps protect the tip.

Always solder in an area with good **ventilation**. You'll notice little wisps of smoke when you heat up your solder. The smoke comes from the rosin in the solder. Rosin is made from pine trees. It can make people with pine allergies uncomfortable and even trigger asthma attacks. Since the smoke is very light, running a fan in the room where you are working is usually enough to keep it from bothering anyone. A kitchen table is a good place to solder. Most kitchens have a vent fan above the stove. Turning it on will help clear the air as you work. Make sure the air blows away from you, though. If it blows toward you, it could make the wire you are trying to solder move.

Tinning an Iron

If your soldering iron has a brand-new tip, you should melt a thin coat of solder onto the tip before using it. This process is called tinning. Tinning your soldering iron's tip will help it conduct heat more evenly and keep it from wearing out. You should start and end each soldering session by tinning the tip. You also need to tin some components before using them.

To tin a soldering iron's tip, plug in the iron and let it get nice and hot. While you are waiting, soak your sponge in water and squeeze it out. It should be damp but not sopping wet. If you don't have a soldering iron stand with a sponge holder, place the sponge in a little dish so you don't get water all over your table. The dish should be made of a material that would not melt if it came in contact with the heat of the soldering iron.

Touch your sponge to the tip of the soldering iron. When the iron is hot enough, it will sizzle and steam as soon as it touches the sponge. Then you're ready to go. Tinning the iron's tip has just two steps:

- Wipe the tip of your soldering iron on the damp sponge to clean it. Wait a few seconds for the iron to return to being hot again.
- Touch the end of your coil of solder to the tip of the iron. The solder will immediately melt and flow evenly over the tip.

Remember: Tin the tip again when you are done soldering. Storing the iron with a tinned tip will keep it working better for longer. Even if you take great care of them, all soldering iron tips eventually wear out. A tip should be replaced when it turns dark and feels rough, pitted, or lumpy.

That's it! Now you're ready to start soldering.

WARNING

The tip of a soldering iron gets very hot—around 750 degrees Fahrenheit (400 degrees Celsius)! That is almost twice as hot as your kitchen oven gets at its highest temperature. Always pay attention to where you place the tip of your soldering iron, as it can easily burn clothes, furniture, and your skin.

Soldering

Gather your tools, heat up your iron, and make sure your sponge is damp. Once the iron's tip is hot enough to make the damp sponge sizzle, you're ready to start. Soldering has four steps:

- **Connect the components:** Make a solid connection between the parts you want to solder. This often means twisting two wires together. If you are adding components to a **circuit board**, it might involve sliding the component's **lead** through the appropriate hole in the circuit board. A lead is the wire "leg" that sticks out from a component. Bend that lead to one side after you thread it through, so it is making contact with the copper pad on the underside of the board.

- **Heat the joint:** Wipe the iron's tip clean on your damp sponge. Touch it to the joint, or connection, between your parts. This will cause the components to heat up, but it will not melt them.

- **Apply solder:** Touch the solder to the heated joint while keeping the iron in contact with the joint. Do not touch the solder itself with the hot tip of the soldering iron! Forcing hot solder onto a cold

Apply solder to a heated joint while keeping the soldering iron in contact with the joint.

component makes a bad joint. Solder will flow smoothly into a hot joint on its own. Don't use too much solder. Melt just enough to join the pieces together.

- **Cool and snip:** Once the joint is cool, snip off any extra wire that is poking out. Do not wiggle or blow on the joint as the solder cools. This won't speed things up. Rather, it will cause a bad joint to form.

A good solder joint is smooth and shiny. It has enough solder to cover the connection of the components, but not so much that the solder looks like a round bead or droplet. If you are soldering to a circuit board, the joint will look like a little volcano with the component's lead sticking out of it.

Joints that are dull, lumpy, or clumpy are called cold joints. They don't hold up well. They are usually the result of forcing hot solder onto cold wires, removing the iron too quickly once the solder starts to melt, or wiggling a wire while the solder is still soft. You can fix a cold joint by reheating it and maybe adding a little bit of solder.

Tinning Components

Small components with thin leads will heat and solder very quickly. Larger pieces of metal—such as thick wires or the **terminals** on a switch—heat more slowly and take longer to solder. This is a challenge when you connect something small, such as an **LED** (which is like a small lightbulb), to one of these bigger parts. The solution is to give the larger part its own coating of solder before trying to connect it to anything else. This is called tinning the component.

You need to strip the plastic from a wire's tips because you cannot solder metal to plastic. The plastic would melt!

When you solder the smaller component to the tinned component, the layer of solder you added will melt immediately and form a good joint without overheating the smaller component.

Tinning the terminals on a switch is easy. Just use your soldering iron to heat the terminal until solder melts onto it on its own. Tinning the ends of the wire requires a few more steps:

- **Strip:** Strip off 0.25 to 0.5 inch (0.5 to 1.25 centimeters) of the plastic insulation protecting the wire.

- **Twist:** Use your fingers to twist the loose strands of metal wire together.
- **Heat:** Wipe off the tip of your soldering iron. Use it to heat the twisted wires. Be patient. It takes a little

Fixing Mistakes

Did you accidentally connect an LED the wrong way around? Do you have a damaged component that needs to be replaced? Don't worry. You can use your soldering iron to desolder joints. Heat the solder on the joint just enough for it to begin flowing. Now you can carefully pull the components apart.

Things get a bit trickier if you are desoldering a component that's soldered to a circuit board or components that have several connections. In these situations, you should use a desoldering tool along with your iron. Follow these steps:

- Heat the joint: Touch the tip of the iron to the soldered joint you want to remove. The solder will eventually begin to melt.
- Suck the solder up: Use your desoldering tool to suck up as much solder as you can. Blow the solder out of the tool and onto your soldering sponge.
- Repeat: Continue until the solder is mostly gone.
- Separate: Let the joint and component cool. Now you can use a pair of needle-nose pliers to wiggle the component free.

A desoldering tool can also be used to remove a solder bridge. A solder bridge is a place where hot solder has accidentally flowed between two components. Just heat the unwanted solder and suck it up.

longer to heat stranded wire than it does to heat the lead of a **resistor** or an LED.

- **Solder:** While holding the iron in place, touch your solder to the twisted wire. The solder should immediately melt and soak right into the twisted wires. If the solder doesn't melt quickly, take it away and heat the wire for a little longer before trying again.

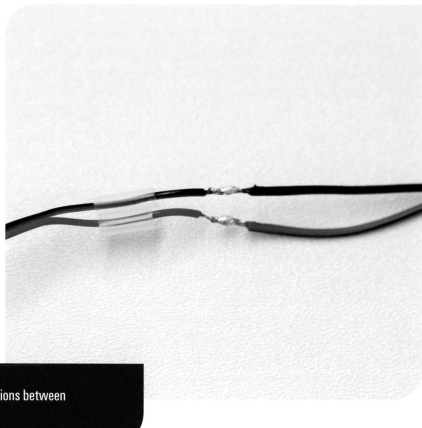

Solder helps make connections between wires secure.

Chapter 4

Building an LED Flashlight

You can use your new soldering skills to make repairs, such as replacing a broken battery clip in a remote control. You can also use your skills to build devices from kits. Once you have practiced a little, you can build projects from scratch using designs you find online or in books. Building an LED flashlight is a good first project. The parts are easy to work with, and the circuit is easy to understand.

The word *circuit* is related to the word *circle*. The idea is that electricity needs to be able to travel out of a battery, around the entire circuit, and back to the battery. When your LED flashlight is turned on, electricity is able to travel over the switch, through a resistor (which controls the electricity and protects the LED), and into the LED. Then the electricity returns to the battery. As long as the electricity can flow around the circuit, the LED will glow. When the switch is turned off, the circuit is broken. No electricity can flow, so there is no light.

Now is the time to ask yourself what kind of enclosure—or box—you want for your project. Most flashlight enclosures are tubes. You could use a mailing tube, a spice jar, or a piece of plastic pipe as your enclosure. You could also use a small gift box, a LEGO creation, an old stuffed animal, or a dried gourd. When you build something yourself, you get to decide what it looks like. The possibilities are limitless!

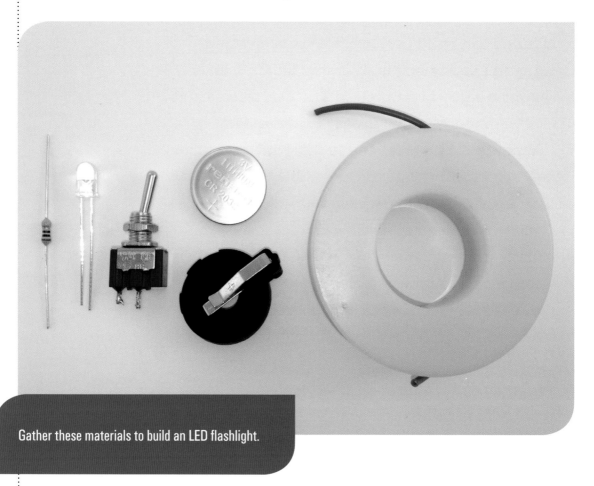

Gather these materials to build an LED flashlight.

Supplies (shown on page 24):

- A high-brightness white LED (RadioShack part #276-017)
- A 10Ω resistor (RadioShack part #271-1101; the stripes on this resistor are brown-black-black)
- A small toggle switch (RadioShack part #275-612) or push-button switch (RadioShack part #275-1547)
- A 3-volt CR2032 "button cell" battery
- A CR2032 battery holder (RadioShack part #270-009)
- 24-gauge insulated "hook-up" wire
- Enclosure

Want a different color flashlight? Most RadioShack stores also stock red LEDs and yellow LEDs. If you decide to go with red or yellow, you will need to use a 22Ω resistor instead (part #271-1103; it will have red-red-black stripes).

As always, the first step is to get your tools ready. Ask an adult to help plug in your soldering iron, get your sponge damp, and gather your other tools. Once the iron is hot enough to make the sponge sizzle, you're ready to tin your iron and get started.

- **Prepare your wires:** Cut three pieces of wire. Each should be about 3 inches long (7.5 cm). Strip ½ inch (1.25 cm) of insulation from the ends of each wire. Twist and tin the exposed metal ends.
- **Prepare your switch:** Tin the two terminals on your switch. Solder one wire to each terminal.
- **Prepare your LED:** Solder one lead of the resistor (it doesn't matter which) to the longer lead of the LED. Solder one end of the last piece of insulated wire to the other lead of the LED.

The LED's longer lead connects to the resistor (bottom). The shorter lead connects to the insulated wire (top).

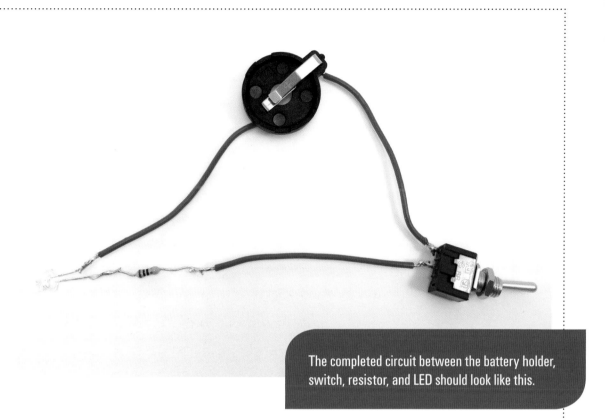

The completed circuit between the battery holder, switch, resistor, and LED should look like this.

- **Assemble your switch and LED:** Solder one wire from the switch (it doesn't matter which one) to the only lead that's left on the resistor.
- **Add power:** You're almost done! Your battery holder has two small terminals, or metal posts, on the bottom. One is near the center, and one is on the edge. Solder the remaining wire that is connected to the switch to the terminal on the edge of the battery holder. Solder the other free wire (the one connected directly to the LED) to the other terminal on the battery clip.

- **Check your work and test your project:** Take a careful look at your solder joints. Is each one a good joint? Are they all shiny and smooth? Is everything wired correctly? If everything looks

Looking for Trouble

If your project isn't working, it's time for a little **troubleshooting**. Start by removing the battery. Check to make sure you wired everything properly. In this project, the LED and battery are the only two parts that could be backward. The LED is the trickiest one. If you look at the LED carefully, you'll see that there is a flat spot on the edge of the base. This flat spot is on the same side of the LED as the shorter LED lead. It should go to a wire that connects directly to the battery. The other lead is the one that's connected to the resistor. Once you're sure that all of the components are connected properly, check each solder joint. If any of them are dull or lumpy, try reheating them and letting them cool again.

Finally, look for short circuits. These are places where electricity is able to take a shortcut and skip part of the circuit. Short circuits can be caused when bare wires or joints are touching each other. They can also happen when solder has dribbled between two nearby components and created a solder bridge. Look for solder bridges between the terminals of the switch and on the LED. If you find one, just heat it with your iron. This should draw away the extra solder. You can also suck up this extra solder by using a desoldering tool.

good, install your battery. The little plus sign should be on the top side of the battery. Now flick the switch. Let there be light! Wrap some electrical tape around each joint. This will keep the joints from touching each other and breaking your circuit. Now you can install the assembled circuit into your enclosure.

No matter how simple or complicated your projects are, you can use these techniques to bring your ideas to life.

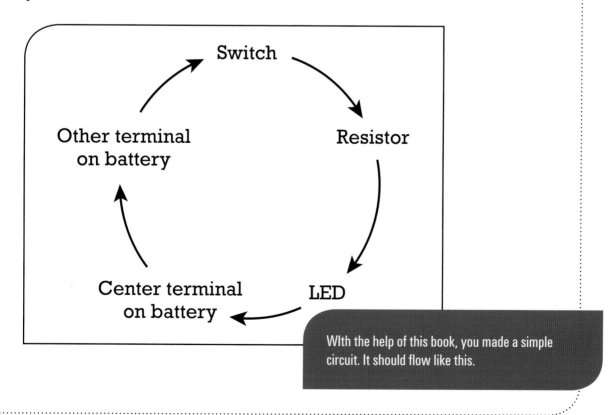

With the help of this book, you made a simple circuit. It should flow like this.

Glossary

circuit board (SIR-kit BORD) a thin sheet onto which electrical components are mounted

circuits (SIR-kits) complete paths for electrical current

components (kuhm-POH-nuhnts) parts of a larger whole, especially a machine or a system

conducts (kuhn-DUKTS) allows electricity to pass through

insulation (in-suh-LAY-shuhn) material that does not allow electricity to pass through

lead (LEED) a wire that helps electricity flow more effectively through a component

LED (ELL-EE-DEE) a small light that can be switched on or off; LED stands for "light-emitting diode."

maker (MAY-kur) someone who invents or creates something

resistor (ruh-ZIS-tur) an electrical component that reduces the flow of electricity in a circuit

soldering (SAH-dur-ing) joining pieces of metal by putting a small amount of heated, melted metal between them

terminals (TUR-muh-nuhlz) sturdy metal parts that connect a switch, jack, or other piece of hardware to the other components in a circuit

troubleshooting (TRUHB-uhl-shoo-ting) finding and solving problems with a project

ventilation (ven-tuh-LAY-shuhn) the process of allowing fresh air into a place and letting stale air out

Find Out More

BOOKS

Mims, Forrest M., III. *Getting Started in Electronics*. Lincolnwood, IL: Master Publishing, 2003.

Nelson, David Erik. *Snip, Burn, Solder, Shred: Seriously Geeky Stuff to Make with Your Kids*. San Francisco: No Starch Press, 2010.

WEB SITES

Instructables
www.instructables.com
This site hosts free illustrated instructions for many soldering projects.

Maker Shed
www.makershed.com
Purchase supplies, kits, tools, and instructions for a variety of DIY projects.

Soldering Is Easy! Here's How to Do It
http://mightyohm.com/files/soldercomic/FullSolderComic_EN.pdf
Read this online comic book to learn more soldering tips and tricks.

Index

About the Author

David Erik Nelson lives in Ann Arbor, Michigan, with his lovely wife, tolerable children, and aging poodle. He is the author of *Snip, Burn, Solder, Shred: Seriously Geeky Stuff to Make with Your Kids*. His science fiction stories have appeared in *The Magazine of Fantasy & Science Fiction, Asimov's Science Fiction*, and a variety of anthologies. Find him online at *www.davideriknelson.com*.